Make your life bright and creative

The Simple Guide to Raise Your Self-Esteem And to Find Yourself

Your   Gift

I wanted to show my appreciation that you support my work so I've put together a free gift for you.

http://bonusfreebook.org/

Just visit the link above to download it now.

I know you will love this gift.

If you like this book, you can see and buy my other books on this link:

ALL BOOKS OLIVER SMITH HERE

Thank you for attention!

With love,

OLIVER SMITH

Contents

INTRODUCTION

In today's world where every success is attached to an invention and a fresh initiative, everyone has to know himself and work on himself to make something work out. There are too many people blundering around in the dark looking for the switch to success when they only need look for the switch for creativity and then sit back and watch as success pours in. Discovery of one's authentic self is the bedrock of all success. Every victory, every landmark event and every story of greatness was birthed out of the mind of men that discovered themselves, who never lived on critics' opinions or listened to what naysayers had to say.

Can creativity be taught or learned? The answer to this question is in the affirmative. For many years, conventional wisdom held that a person was either creative or not. Nevertheless, most of today's research shows that any person can learn through techniques and behavior to become creative. Embedded in every mind is a spectacular ability, the ability to bring out an inner glow and make an individual shine brighter. Deep within every soul is that creative ability. Creativity is the power to create, an ability to make things happen. A creative life can only be achieved by knowing and acting upon this inner ability.

This book is written not only to give the reader the knowledge of creativity but to make you understand what it takes to have a creative life, what you need to know about yourself and the conscious effort required to put into making the light shine. It will help you see yourself and raise your self-esteem; you will stop looking down on yourself, you will also find a way to make your life creative and worth appreciating.

To bring out the creative power that you have, it would be a good thing answer the question:

"Who am I?"

The world wants to know what you have seen in yourself that makes you think you can be relevant, appreciated and known, but the first challenge is within you. If you have the right kind of belief in yourself, the opinions of others cannot negate yours. Your self-esteem is a major determinant of the amount of success you can achieve.

If you are yet to know what to put your time into, going through a time of confusion in that which you are doing, constantly failing in seeing your ability, then this book is for you. You have heard enough of great stories, seen enough of exclusively creative works, it is time to create your own to have the world listen to you and achieve beyond your wildest dreams. All you need is already within you, it's just need to reach inside yourself and bring out the creativity within you.

CHAPTER ONE

CREATIVITY IN YOUR LIFE

"Our fantasy is our everything. It is the look-ahead of life`s charms."
— *Albert Einstein*

Besides basic survival, every other human being on earth is in a race against himself to be successful. Every single individual wants to be able to complete his goals and live his dreams every single waking hour is filled with people striving and trying their best to leave a mark, a legacy to be remembered for. Every minute, the majority of the world's population tries to realize their potentials by working hard to the best of their abilities.

Yet, only very few people ever get to achieve true success and break through the glass ceiling. Only a few numbers of people will get to experience their dreams and reach the promised life. Too many people fail at what they are trying their hands at and the reason is not too farfetched. Most people do the same things the same way everybody else is doing them and expect different, nay great results. Things don't just work that way any longer. If you must experience utopia and true success, you need to be creative. You need to be able to tap into your mind's power of imagination and use it to your full advantage. There are simply no other shortcuts to success. You are either with the crowd, doing the same things they are doing, in the same manner. Or you may choose to be different and find ingenious solutions to knotty issues. The truth of the matter is that the world is so technologically advanced these days that the simple things are counting for less and less. Nobody is becoming a successful person from finding simple solutions to simple problems. You need to be able to tap into that reservoir of creativity that runs beneath everyone's consciousness and use it to become different.

What is creativity?

Creativity is at once both hard and easy to define. In its simplest forms, it envisages being able to devise plans that aim to ingenuously find solutions to problems that have so far defied common solutions. There is no denying the fact that many problems can prove to be very hard nuts to crack and it is only by going a level higher through reasoning that you can cope with them. Creativity does not just apply to problems though; it is an entirely fresh way of living your life from day today in such a manner that it never gets too dull or uninspiring. It involves finding new ways of doing things. There is an excitement to discovering or trying out new things and creativity supplies this excitement in huge quantities.

How to think creative

How exactly can you begin to apply creativity to your thinking? In the first place, I will have you know that creativity is a function of the mind. It is not a product of external forces, circumstances or conditions. Creativity will always shine out from within a creative person. The circumstances and conditions don't really matter. Our mind is the most powerful organ in the body; it not only controls the brain and all conscious action, it also determines our thought process and approach towards almost everything in life. By extension, it determines just how successful we are going to be. To think creatively starts from acknowledging that you need to find ways around every obstacle on your path and introduce novelty into your life. Creativity is a process in the mind and to think creatively, you need to open your mind, free yourself up and look for solutions in improbable places.

New ideas – new life

In the perpetual flux of the world, change is the only constant and creativity represents change. Creativity means that you constantly have new ideas and suggestions about how to do new things. Creativity means you are forever ahead of the game and always one foot ahead of everybody. This is a very important factor in creating your success. Maya Angelou said: "It is impossible to deplete creativity. The more you use, the more you have." The more you become creative and sprout up new ideas, the better your life changes. Nobody can become more creative and not experience tremendous positive changes in every facet of his life. It is important for you to use your creativity to create a new life that can help you strike success faster.

With creativity, you can find solutions to questions you had no idea existed. A creative individual's mind is forever the web of new ideas and inspiration. When you learn to open your mind to accept new ideas, you create an entirely new being different from the old you. With creativity firmly implanted in you, you would find it impossible to continue to live life the way you were. With creativity coursing through you, you will become a newer, better version of yourself and find it easier to maximize your potential and achieve beyond the limit of your abilities.

Break your borders

Everybody has one little voice at the back of his head preaching caution and discretion. This little voice consistently advocates for safety and caution first. It is the voice that tells you to exercise undue patience rather than strike the iron while it is still hot. It is the same voice that asks that you stay with the pack on the well-worn path rather than forge yourself a new route to success. This voice tries to limit us from possible failure by asking us to stick to try and tested methods, which invariably is what every other person is doing.

However, there is no safety in sticking to the crowd, only obscurity and mediocrity. If you do not take risks, you cannot gain the higher ground against failure. You need to break your mind out of the shackles of negativity. You need to rid your mind of that little voice that serves as your limiting factor. You need to break out of the "follow the crowd syndrome". Allow your mind to roam free and about, unhindered by a parochial societal view, fears or artificial limits. Who decided a certain task wasn`t done? Who told you it cannot be you to achieve the impossible? There is no problem too big for you; you only need a new angle to look at it from. You only need to approach all issues with a clean slate and the belief that it can be fixed. Once you have this belief, you are good to go. Once you set your mind free and remove all borders to reasoning, success cannot be too far away. Break the borders and allow yourself tap into the tank of creativity within you.

The unstoppable power of imagination

Imagination is the food of creativity. The ability to look beyond the physical and obvious nature of any task or item is a critical part of creativity. You need to be able to visualize your efforts as if they have succeeded. You need to draw pure, undiluted inspiration to see what others do not see. You need to open up your inner eye and use it to great advantage. You need to be able to imagine how one plus one may equally three. Imagination cannot even be taught, learned or studied; it is already inbuilt in everybody. The only problem is that it comes with a limiting seal that reduces your access to your core of imagination. Break this seal, open your borders and allow your creative genius to pour out from within you

Creativity is a must if you have the plan to succeed. You must be resourceful, highly dynamic and possess that ability to spot what is missing in the equation. You must be able to proffer something genuinely different from what every other person is holding in their hands. Always rememberthat a creative person is a successful person, and successful people are always extra creative. They didn't just sit and wait for things to happen, they went out there to make them happen.

CHAPTER TWO

YOU ARE UNIQUE

"Being the best of the best and number one is great. Being unique is greater, because you are the only one."
-Anonymous

Estimates suggest that there are over 7 billion people in the world. That translates to 7 billion goals, histories, profiles, likes, dislikes, failures, hopes, expectations, and desires. Every one of these people is **unique.** Each one of them has been equipped with a unique set of strengths and opportunities to make sense and progress of whatever pursuit, goals or aspirations they may seek to have. Everybody exists in a unique aura of personal consciousness that can help achieve his/her goal.

But unfortunately, 99% of the entire population is unaware of this. They spend the vast majority of their time casting envious glances at what they expect to be perfect lives around them, oblivious of the envious glances they are getting in turn. They under-appreciate their own abilities and magnify the strengths and opportunities that other people around them seem to have. The result is that they end up missing the point of life; the fact that we are all born different and made different to be able to satisfy our unique and particular needs. They omit the fact that they have been given the ideal life and tools to make a success out of their own life.

Your inner power

Let us be brutally honest: you might never be as strong as your friend, or have as much wealth as your brother or record the success of Steve Jobs but that is not because you cannot have the body of your friend, run your brother's business or get the chances Steve Jobs had. You simply cannot achieve these things because you are not your brother, friend or Steve Jobs. You are **YOU!!!** And there is no escaping that fact.

Wherever you go, at any particular moment, you remain yourself and the best possible thing you can do is to acknowledge this. After recognizing this fact, you can then work on unleashing the inner power within you. Of course, you have your own special inner power, Superman or Batman-like. Your mind contains a driving force that when activated cannot be stopped by the vagaries of time or frustration. When you have decided to engage this positively domineering power of your mind, you can be sure that the road in front of you is going to become a lot smoother. I not because the potholes and bumps within the road are going to disappear, but because your vehicle now has a stronger, bigger engine propelling it along the path to success.

Find your strengths

There is no need to hide from your weaknesses because everybody has them. There is no point in trying to judge yourself based on your weaknesses, though. They are a constant part of you and you just need to learn to deal with them. How can you deal with your weaknesses? Contrary to popular opinions that recognize weaknesses as a fault, they are not entirely pessimistic. If you become informed enough, you will realize that your weaknesses can aid you magnify your strength. Instead of your weaknesses as an excuse not to make a huge effort, exploit your strengths as a prop to reach beyond your head.

Consider yourself critically and find out what you do best. Find out the things you can do at a level that most people cannot. These are your strengths and you need to tap into them to experience tremendous and geometric progress. Learn to fine-tune your strengths to further hone them to perfection. Do not leave them in a raw state. Develop your strengths and use them to serve as a base for launching your success. Do not let your weaknesses to weigh you down. Instead, use your strengths appropriately to generate success.

Be proud of your victories and defeats

Victory is sweet, defeats can be bitter and painful but both are equally as important as the other. You can learn as much from your defeats as your victories but you do not need to try to forget your defeats too. Naturally, victories are sweeter and are therefore more pleasurable to recollect. In fact, recollection of your past victories can give you an impetus to try out new things. It can fuel your confidence and give you the self-belief you need to make a difference. A victory can serve as a mental stepping block to better things.

Nevertheless, your failures happen for a single reason for you to learn and make a better attempt. Do not fall into the trap of seeing your failures as an admission of the fact that you are not good enough. Far from it, you are even much better than those that do not make an attempt. Your failures are designed to be a safety limit for you. They are designed to build an alarm system that will warn you each time you are taking too dangerously a risk. Both victories and defeats are important. The former to bring a spring into your step and the latter, to provide you with a contrast of how things look on the other side. This would elevate your euphoria when you finally succeed. Take Steve Jobs' advice: "Develop success from misfortunes. Melancholy and misfortune are two of the right stepping stones to be successful".

Listen to your body

Our body is the vessel that holds our mind in place and gives it the needed tools to make an impact. The brain may be important as the organ that controls the body but it needs the body in perfect tip-top shape to be able to obtain anything. Do not understand the importance of good health. The body has many alarm systems that tell you when you are at the edge of your physical and mental limits; listen to these alarms. Do not overwork your body just yet; you have only one. Allow yourself sufficient rest and exercise to keep your body in the right frame of conditions to provide you maximum support during your struggles to become successful.

Never settle for less

Do not compromise your excellence and drive to succeed. Do not commit the ultimate crime of sacrificing your goals for pleasure. Or, even worse, shelve your goals because the prospects in front of you are frightening. Your uniqueness means you deserve everything you want and more besides. Do not undervalue or lower your expectations in the face of adversity.

There is only one of you on earth at this particular moment; nobody else can replace what you represent. Only you have been equipped with the tools to make a success out of your dreams and goals. If at any time you feel like you are getting trampled among the crowds, let the words of Aaron Perlowinspire you: "We are obligated to understand we are unique in this world. There has never been anyone like you because, if there were, there would be no need for you to exist. You are an extremely new thing in creation. Your mission is to comprehend this uniqueness."

CHAPTER THREE

THINK DIFFERENT

"I never made one of my discoveries in the process of rational thinking"
— Albert Einstein

Like I said earlier, our thoughts determine the actions we take and our actions determine the level of success we experience. Therefore, to soar above the majority of people, you need to be extraordinary. And to be extraordinary, you need thinking above the ordinary.. You need to think differently of other people if you do not wish to get the same result every other person is getting too. Every scientific, commercial and technological breakthrough was due to somebody thinking outside the box. Every major success story was due to somebody being bold and creative enough to challenge laid-down norms and rules.

You cannot afford to conform if you want to leave a lasting legacy. You simply do not have that luxury of thinking along the white lines. You must be prepared to dip above and below the lines to create something really special. Rational thinking is only good to a certain limit; like when you are only trying to repeat a feat and not create something new. However, if you have designs, plans and intentions of being the best possible person you can be, then, you need to stop conforming and start existing.

To do this, you need to be able to think wildly and factor in conditions nobody else would even consider. Steve Jobs, Bill Gates and Elon Musk didn't just become super-rich and successful by thinking like every other person. They became so because they dared to think out of conventional limits. They dared to ask the questions every other person could not ask. They chose to dare. Nothing is stopping you too except your mind.

How to be confident

Confidence is a very vital aspect of becoming an individual capable of not only asking the right questions but seeking the solution to the hardest problems around. To be able to think differently, you need to first be trusting of your ability to think. Many people who actually think out of the box, and hit upon a glorious idea often abandon it still due to a lack of enough confidence. Many of them get flustered and cannot even begin to think of the impact of their ideas and discoveries. They dither and allow conditions and factors to change so much that they lose the initial advantage they hold. Confidence though is a product of competence and high levels of self-esteem. You must first attain at least a basic knowledge of what you are trying to do. If you don't, then perhaps your low level of confidence shouldn't surprise you too much. Then, you need to build your esteem and self-worth; you need to trust in your own abilities to be able to hold your head high.

Believe in your success

If anybody can do it, then, it has to be you. If anyone can make an impact, you are the one. You must not just daydream or hope that you can do it; that is not enough. You have to obtain absolute conviction in your ability to succeed. You have to feel like you are already successful. You cannot have any doubts about the outcome of your efforts. You are not permitted to harbor any self-doubts or suspicions about how primed you are to make a difference. You must just believe in the strength of your convictions, the potency of your efforts and the effectiveness of your ability to mark a path out for you.

Dr. Barry Marshallwas convinced that a bacterium, *Helicobacter pylori,* was responsible for stomach ulcers rather than the well-believed theory of high acidity and alkalinity, but he was unable to convince his fellow scientists. He was so confident of his theory that he took a drastic way to prove his theory. He actually drank some *Helicobacter pylori*, developed ulcer proved everybody else wrong and perpetuate his name in medical folklore. He was able to do this because he never doubted himself or his idea. Once he became convinced about the genuineness of his idea, he never paused even once to consider that he might be wrong.

You need to imbibe this spirit too. You need to learn to stick to your guns when you are sure you are on the right way. Many people allow themselves get discouraged by people and opinions; they allow others help them to give up.

Relating to others

Our relationship with the people around us is indeed a great marker of the level of fulfillment we are going to derive in life. There are all kinds of relationships, productive or unproductive, in our life and the ratio we maintain between the productive and unproductive relationships may contribute to either slow you down or provide you with extra support. Learning to live in harmony and peace with the people around you, friends and family, gives you some extra sources of motivation, strength, and courage to do the needful. Learn to relate to others in ways that can bring the best out of you and them.

Marking your own creative route out

It was Robin S. Sharma who said: "All great thinkers are ridiculed at the beginning but in the long run revered." It couldn't have been more right. To become a great thinker and success, you need to develop a thick skin to the reactions of people. You need to be able to decide on the manner to approach your goals and then stay true to your decision. There is no point in thinking differently from other people if you don't put your ideas into action. It is an acute waste of your time if you cannot translate your thoughts into productive action. It is not just important that you think differently, you need to also use your superior thinking process to develop a well-detailed plan designed to bring the best out of you.

Stay curious

Curiosity is a great part of success and constant, consistent improvement. You have been like a sponge when it comes to keeping up to date with the variables of your plan and consequently success. You need to be aware of happenings, past and present that can hinder or help your efforts. You need to be hungry to check all ends out. Do not allow the fear of being proven wrong hold you back. Information is power: stay curious at all times to extract as much of it as you can get. Do not be afraid of the next step: be eager to take it and be done with it. Tom Huddleston said: "We never know what's approaching because it could be everything or just nothing. We step over some difficulties, and then some day we look back and we've climbed a mountain".

CONCLUSION

Why are names like Walt Disney, Lou Macari, Muhammed Ali, Celine Dion, Jay-Z, Cristiano Ronaldo, Henry Ford, Leonardo Da Vinci, Beethoven, Messi, Tiger Woods and Revered Martin Luther King revered across the world? Obviously, they were all very successful in their chosen pursuits, but what was the secret of their success? What did they possess in abundance that every other Tom and Harry on the street lack?

Each and every one of these names including other successful individuals that have left their lasting marks on the world all had the three weapons of creativity, confidence and a sense of uniqueness to guide them around the darkness of obscurity. Successful people never lay back; it is almost a taboo for them. They never sit around and sulk at what life has thrown at them; they either get up and use it to unimaginable success or stand up and go take some more for themselves.

To be creative is to be along the path to success. It is the most important asset a man can be bestowed with. It is the master key that opens all doors that lead to success. To become truly creative though, you need to be guided by a clear identity of what you are and what you want from life. You have to be bold enough to ask life for sugar and a container for your lemonade when it throws you only lemons. If life doesn't give you sugar, then, you need to learn to find sugar elsewhere. Do not just sit down with your lemons in hand waiting for life. Get out there; release the shackles from your mind, free your soul, break the barriers and soar to success. I have this little quote pasted onto my bathroom mirror every morning where I can see it. Conceivably you should too. It says:

"Some people who are crazy enough to believe they can change the worldreally can do it." (Rob Siltanen)